Matters of the Soul

365 Spiritual and Inspirational Quotes,
in no particular order

By Bryan D. Johnson

i

Matters of the Soul

Introduction

I wrote this book over the course of five years, after having had a transformational experience that changed my life for the better.

The quotes would come to me at random times when my mind was clear of the clutter and free to receive what the universe was sending to me. I would write it down on my phone, send it to myself, and put it in a Word document. I finally decided to write this book in the Summer of 2019.

My father, Jeffrey Johnson, helped me edit this book from start to finish. Debbie Trent was the first person to tell me to write a book in the Fall of 2014 and has been a constant supporter.

I am grateful that God granted me the gift to receive and write these quotes, and I am happy to share them with you. Thanks for reading this book. I hope you enjoy it.

Sincerely,

Bryan D. Johnson

Acknowledgements

I would like to thank Gulf Breeze Recovery and all the staff for helping me find my true self. Without their loving support, I would not have stayed married and tapped into a new talent that allowed me to write this book. Joe Bailey has done an amazing job training the staff, and he and I go way back to 1989 when he tried to help me as a counselor in Minnesota. Funny how he reappeared in my life, and I am grateful for that.

I would like to say a special thank you to the late Sydney Banks, who discovered the Three Principles of Mind, Consciousness and Thought in the early 1970s. He was a common man who had an enlightening experience and wanted to share it with the world. I was fortunate to have seen him speak about six times, but I wasn't ready to hear the message. However, his teachings were being taught at Gulf Breeze Recovery, and I finally heard the truth.

The saying is true; when the student is ready, the teacher will appear. I listen to his CDs regularly and still get something out of it. His contribution to the world is immeasurable. My gratitude towards that man is immense.

When I left Gulf Breeze Recovery, I was matched up with Lisa Portinga, an aftercare provider. She has been an invaluable mentor through the good and bad times. I am truly grateful for her help and guidance.

Finally, I want to acknowledge my family. My wife and children are a constant source of love and joy. My wife supported me in writing this book and encouraged me along the way. My mother and father have always believed in me and loved me, no matter what. My brother has seen the growth in me since Gulf Breeze, and our relationship is closer, even though we live in different states.

Forward

As a child, I was fascinated by the Greek legend of the Phoenix, an amazing bird that had the capacity to arise from its own ashes, live again and flourish.

As an adult, I have been lucky enough to see that people have that same capacity – the resiliency and ability to rise above what can appear to be impossible challenges.

When I first met Bryan, I was the Clinical Director at Gulf Breeze Recovery, a residential substance abuse treatment center in the Florida panhandle. Although I believe with my whole being that everyone has health inside, Bryan had it very well hidden. I hoped he would be open to hearing what we were sharing and would come to realize that he wasn't broken and that he had all the wisdom he needed to navigate his life.

We all do, but sometimes we forget it. And some people believe in their broken-ness more than they believe in their capacity to heal.

When he arrived at Gulf Breeze Recovery, Bryan had completed his crash and burn phase. He had hit his rock bottom, had destroyed his marriage and didn't even seem to have the energy to care.

Trying to find the right words to describe the Bryan I first met is difficult. He was always polite, he would answer questions if asked directly, but with no emotion, an almost blankness. He wasn't rebellious and never broke the rules or pushed boundaries. It was almost as if he had retreated so deeply inside himself that he just preferred to be left alone. Of course, we wouldn't leave him alone, so he sat through classes, group sessions and individual sessions with his assigned therapist, and did all the things we asked him to do without complaint.

Slowly, changes started to occur, and he began to show some interest in what we were teaching. He began reading more books from our library, especially those written by Sydney Banks, who he had met many years before. He started to show an intellectual understanding of what we taught, but I could see that he didn't really "feel" it.

Bryan's transformation may not have been quite as spectacular as the Phoenix taking flight from the ashes, but it was just as amazing. When Bryan had his "Aha" moment, everything about him changed! He jumped to a level of understanding about himself and the world that is beyond description.

Bryan started to say things that are best described as pure wisdom about human nature. He had emotions and wasn't ashamed to shed tears of joy or laugh out loud. I encouraged him to write down some of the things he was saying. I told him to keep them for the book he would write someday.

Knowing that he had changed from the person he was before, Bryan was determined to reclaim his family and rebuild his marriage, but he also had the wisdom to recognize that the process might take a while. He knew that he would have to be patient. It did take a while, but his wife recognized the transformation in Bryan, and together, they began to build a stronger relationship than ever before.

After Bryan left Gulf Breeze Recovery, we stayed in touch. When he had been home for about a year or so, I asked him and his wife to be speakers for the guests at Gulf Breeze Recovery on Valentine's Day, and they graciously shared their story.

Small postings that Bryan shared on Facebook continued to surprise me with their depth, simplicity, beauty, and pure wisdom. More than once, I encouraged him to put them together and write a book that he could share with the world.

Recently, Bryan told me that he had written his book. He allowed me to read it and asked me to write the foreword for it. I told him I would be honored.

Debbie Trent

Licensed Mental Health Counselor

God loves us too much
to not give us everything we need.

God wouldn't leave us up
a creek without a paddle.

The ego is just a facade,
a false front, and not the real you.

Love is the power that
lets us bloom like a flower.

Truth needs no justification.

Being spiritually awakened to any degree doesn't make
you exempt from being human.

The clouds of negativity can't affect the blue sky of happiness.

Information won't make you wise. Wisdom is drawn from the inside out.

No amount of stress is healthy.

Being hard on yourself is like suffocating yourself and trying to breathe at the same time.

Everything comes from the same Source.   There really is
only one cook in the kitchen.

We are looking for God, but God **is** everything. So, in essence, we are looking for ourselves.

The intangible is tangible.

We all need compassion...for others, and especially for ourselves.

Taking responsibility for our life is positive and empowering. It's very different from blaming ourselves, which is negative and self-defeating.

When Insights come, just marinate in the beautiful feeling without putting it into words.

The beautiful feeling that comes is more important than the words.

If you clear your mind,
you will feel divine.

There is no prerequisite needed
to meditate.

The road less traveled is
from the head to the heart.

If you get into a debate about Truth, you are missing the point.

You don't have to change your life
to change your life.

There's enough love in us to make it through our entire life.

We can't see the beauty in life
until we see it in ourselves first.

Let a flood of gratitude wash over you and carry you away.

By doing nothing, we are doing something. That's how we let go. Our thoughts are free to pass by.

It's a paradox.

Teacher: All the answers you seek lie in a silent mind.
Student: I have a question.
Teacher: I'm afraid you've missed the point.

Great minds think alike because all wisdom comes from the same source.

You are innocent. Lighten up on yourself, and you do not deserve self-criticism.

Love is always enough.

The path is always there...
it just needs to be cleared.

It's nice when a glimmer of truth shines through, and the intellect has no argument for it, and we feel peaceful.

Gratitude is a complete, fulfilling feeling.

It's good wanting to be you when you grow up, because you are okay just the way you are.

You don't have to be perfect
to be perfect.

Sometimes, we need some liquid plumber for the mind to unclog things.

We only see whatever we illuminate.

The intellect is the wrong tool to examine one's life.

We must refuse to be a victim of our own thinking.   Day by day and moment by moment.

The ego is a distorted lens through which to view life.

It's smart to follow your heart.

Once we have found our way home, we may go astray from time to time. But we always find our way back.

You don't need to know the details to be okay.

The best gift we can ever give is
our presence.

God knows that we are stronger than we think we are.
That's why we never get more than we can handle.

When the mind is still like a calm lake, our image of reality
is clearer just like the reflection of a lake.

Our essence is not of this world.

Maybe the details have already been worked out on your behalf.

Analyzing your thoughts and moods is a formula for compounding them.

Positive thinking is like going outside on a cloudy day and saying it's sunny. Truth is going outside on a cloudy day and knowing the sun is always shining behind the clouds.

Love reigns in higher planes.

You certainly can look too far for truth, but you can't look too closely.

Life itself is like a really good rich cake; it's good all on
its own. There is no need for the icing on top.

It's good to have a case of problem amnesia. You forget to worry, forget to be sad, forget to be angry, etc.

We have never been in this moment before.

Love is the only thing that is real.

God wants to hang out with us every day. It's up to us to clear our minds and submit our will to the greater. The connection is felt through love.

God is the only friend we have
that is always around and
is wherever we are.

We are already in this moment, so we might as well enjoy it or at least make the best of it.

Trying to change a behavior without changing that
which created it just doesn't work.

If you're going to do something foolish, at least do it mindfully.

God gave us gifts to use, not to lose.

Love is either unconditional,
or it isn't love.

Moods come and go; there's no need to stop the flow.

Love can make anything tolerable. Sometimes, it even makes things disappear.

Apply love every day and reapply frequently. It's like sunscreen for the soul.

The beauty is in seeing the beauty. It always shines from the inside out.

A little bit better is still better.

Stop earning credits at the school of hard knocks and enroll in the school of Love and Understanding. Life is much better there, and learning is easier.

Adults are just as innocent as children; we just lose sight of that.

God answers our calls 24/7
and always has time for us.

It would be hard to drive if you were always looking in the rearview mirror. Likewise, it's hard to function in a healthy state of mind if we are always looking at the past.

Some files (thoughts) are best to be deleted and left in the trash bin.

Life is like an obstacle course...focusing on the negative adds more obstacles.

There are only two sides to a coin. You can only look at one side at a time.

Being in the Now is like an unexpected bonus. It is not a
goal.

Love is the best mood-altering drug there is.

Happiness is a current event.

Love and understanding are truthfully enough to get you
through anything with grace.

We are the complete package.

An insight is like an intermission from a game.

The more love,
the more understanding of life.

Play the game of life as if it were a practice game. Relax,
make mistakes, and take risks.

God doesn't make incomplete packages.

It's normal to be abnormal.

90

Our ego is like a protester at our own pep rally. We just must ignore it and pay attention to the cheers of the crowd.

The ego needs permission.

You enrich the lives around you
just by **being yourself**.

Think outside of that space between your ears.

Being unhappy is optional.

F.E.A.R - Face Everything with Assurance and Resiliency.

Gratitude is not a matter of creating a feeling by the act of counting one's blessings. It's something that washes over us when least expected, and we SEE with LOVE what we already have.

The key to your treasure chest
lies inside.

If you stop adding fuel to a fire, it burns out on its own.

The inner world is hidden, and we look in the outer world for the solution. Until one day, we look inside, and the game is over.

You are not off track. You only think you are.

If you look for a burning bush, you might miss a single flame.

A wise fish knows which is bait and which is real food. Likewise, a wise person knows which thoughts are bait and which thoughts feed the soul.

People can't grow and flourish without **love.**

The only thing we have to fear is our own thinking, only if we take it too seriously.

Thoughts move, that's what they do. They are just like clouds in the sky.

Love is the mother of all beautiful feelings.

A wise sailor knows how to handle the choppy seas and appreciates the calm waters.

You can't get any closer to Truth.
It's wherever you are standing.

Sometimes, what we are looking for is in our own backyard.

There is no end to love and understanding; it's infinite.

We can't lose love, joy and peace... we are love, joy and peace.

We tell ourselves stories to confirm our beliefs about life.

Our beliefs appear like they are made of brick and mortar,
but really, they are more like mirages in the desert.

Wisdom is a knowing without thinking about it.

Love is an overwhelmingly beautiful feeling coming from
our soul, unattached to any person, place, or thing.

The more positive the feeling, the purer are the thoughts. The more negative the feeling, the more impure are the thoughts.

We must be willing to stop the chatter and dare to listen to quietness.   If we do, then we are rewarded with rich, beautiful feelings.

Intellectually knowing your problems come from your
thinking changes nothing.   Having an insight is different; it
changes the whole ballgame.

We can't use the intellect to figure out things that are **matters of the soul.**

You don't have to win a gold medal to be as happy as an Olympian.

A quiet mind speaks more than words.

Raising our level of consciousness solves all our problems
or allows us to accept them.

We never really change; we just shed the layers that were never really us, to begin with.

Soul is pure unconditional love.

Some people have lessons to learn, and some people have lessons to share.

Below is a complete list of everything we can control:

We are all the instruments, and God is the musician.

What we are looking for is not found in our head; it's found in our soul.

We are not tired of the situation; we are tired of our thinking about the situation.

Water in a stream is naturally fresh and pure, whereas water in a pond gets stagnant and dirty. When thoughts naturally flow freely, fresh and pure thoughts can move through us.

The present is the only moment that can be screwed up by two moments that don't exist.

Memorizing metaphors is meaningless.

Confidence is not thinking highly of yourself; it's not thinking about yourself at all.

Beneath the surface, we all really love each other.

Once we find the sweet spot in our soul, we know how to get back there again.

Soul bursts are like fireworks going off inside your soul.

Words can be used to convey a spiritual message, but the words themselves don't contain the message.

We are not very good judges of ourselves, and neither is anybody else.

The divine is a state of no judgement.

We innocently collect baggage along the way, but it's up to us to drop it off.

Gratitude is the way to a higher plane.

If you don't think you have any blessings, hit the refresh button and look again. You might see your blessings with a fresh set of eyes.

Don't argue when you are feeling angry. Wait until you
are in a happy mood, then give it a go.

The only thoughts that are truthful are the ones that make
your heart and soul sing.

The best way to change is don't try to change anything.
Just be yourself.

Letting go or dropping the thought of something works
100% of the time. <u>Trying</u> to let go never works.
Allowing it to pass naturally, does.

In the human assembly line, God didn't leave out anything.
We are all made of the good stuff.

We come pre-programmed with enough wisdom to guide us through every situation in our entire life.

All answers come in the absence of questions. Too many questions actually block the very answers you seek.

We are all allies.

Underneath our earth suit is pure love. That's who we are.

The intellect will never understand what the soul already knows.

All insights originate from Love.

If you want less problems to think about, think less about your problems.

You won't find any solution thinking about your problems.

God is the only teacher, and people are the messengers.

Truth spreads by attraction, not promotion.

The very act of searching for truth stops you from seeing it.

Gratitude nourishes the soul.

Everyone has a higher power in their life, but not everyone realizes it.

It's so unbelievably silly how simple it is. If we don't like
the sound of the tune that's playing in our mind, then
change the channel.
In other words, if we don't like the feeling we are
having, then we can change the thought.

Beware of chronic EMERGENCY SYNDROME; it's an epidemic.
People all over constantly believe their dilemmas are true emergencies requiring immediate responses.

Slow change is better than no change.

Bathe yourself in a deep pool of gratitude. You will feel
spiritually cleansed.

All the gifts we need are in the present.

Love can transcend anything.

Bad thoughts are like a dirty diaper that needs to be changed.

It is never too late...
whatever it is...but start now.

Everything we want lies beyond our limited personal thinking that we unknowingly hold on to for the delusion of comfort. Beyond our own thinking is a love so rich and deep it will fill you and others with a feeling of warmth and wholeness.

Thinking more of yourself won't make you more confident.

Some people try really hard to plan things that can't be planned, like insights.

To relieve mental constipation, stop hoarding your thoughts.

It seems tough to let go when you don't realize you are the one holding on.

Maybe we are all soulmates.

Love is a simple, yet profound answer. If actions are born
of love, then it is hard to go wrong.

The mind can complicate the uncomplicated.

You can set the stage for an insight, but you can't make it happen.

The ego is like a boomerang; it always comes back. When it does come back, we know how to catch and release it again because we are wiser.

A miracle is simply something happening that was never impossible.

If you are feeling your thinking, you are perfectly normal.
You are not broken and don't need to be fixed.

You can't ever really forget TRUTH because it wasn't memorized, to begin with.

Give yourself a break, you are
the only one who can.

Our future will look a lot like our past if we don't find the present.

Our creator wants us to be happy and loves us, that's why our solution was placed within reach, is always available, and lies within all of us.

We don't have to get high to be high on life.

To give and receive love. You can't go wrong with that.
It's so simple yet so profound.

Fuel the fires that create warmth like a campfire, not the ones that burn down a forest.

It is not what is wrong with you that is important; it is what is right with you that is important.

There is no such thing as bad kids or former kids. There are just good people who have gone astray and forgotten their greatness.

What others think of me, and even what I think of myself, really isn't important. It's all a diluted version of reality.

Finding a positive feeling is like fishing. Once you know where the good fishing spots are, it is easier to get your fill.

Wisdom is as versatile of a tool as a Swiss Army knife.

Bask in God's glory.

You are a blessing, whoever you are, just simply by being yourself.

We never really forget how to feel good. We just keep remembering our learned habits, which get in the way of feeling good.

Guilt is like a con man who says if you feel shame about something, you won't do it again. But it is actually a trap that is certain to keep you repeating that behavior.

You don't have to have a still body to have a still mind.

A daily dose of gratitude is good for the attitude.

There is a correlation between our capacity to love and our ability to grow.

Listening to your gut is like having a compass, without which we would be lost.

When we are fully present, no matter what we are doing,
it seems like we are doing it for the first time.

Look within and open a can of awesome sauce and spread it around.

One of the best ways to silence the ego is to just accept it. The ego thrives on constant internal rhetoric. Realizing that we are not our ego, that we are something far greater.

If you want respect, treat everyone, including yourself, with respect.

Blessed are those who know they are blessed.

The richest place in the world is a heart filled with gratitude.

You can find yourself in lostness. Sometimes, we have to go into unchartered territory to find our way home.

You don't have to do something new for it to seem new.

When we are living in our heads, we feel separate. When we are living in our hearts, we feel whole.

Once you find one beautiful feeling, you simultaneously find others because they are all found in the same place, within.

God wouldn't make the answer to life complicated or out of our reach. It's simple; the answer is love, and it's within all of us.

Thoughts just want to be free. Don't hold them prisoner.

Why just dangle your feet in the water when you can jump in?

There is no spiritual destination because you are already there.

Don't trust your thinking when it's stinking.

We are all the same energy in a variety of beautiful costumes.

Gratitude has the power to turn burdens into blessings.

Just like if you go high enough in the atmosphere, there are no more clouds or weather, it is calm and clear. If we raise our level of awareness or consciousness high enough, there is no more ego; there is only purity of thought.

Instead of waiting for a sign from God, be a sign from God.

Thoughts float through our consciousness, like fish in a stream.

It's easy to miss something right in front of you if you are looking in the wrong direction.

The instruction manual for life is found within our soul.

A good teacher must remain teachable.

Life is a treat...savor it!

We are all writing songs, and the universe is playing them exactly the way we write them.

Ignorance of the power of thought; that is the root of the problem.

Seeing life through a diluted thought system is like trying to look through a dirty window.

Trying to fix things from a polluted thought system is like trying to clean with a dirty rag.

Thought pollution is an epidemic.

Thoughts will naturally go away like water down a sink drain when you take the plug off.

God is already giving you a pat on the back, so you might as well give yourself one. Maybe God's even giving you a standing ovation, so give yourself a lot of credit. Only you can do that, and it's no small miracle.

Each piece of a puzzle has its own unique shape and design that only fits into the place it was meant. Everyone wants to fit in, but we already do and there is a spot designed especially for us.

Judgement is a man-made illusion. The only one who has
the authority to judge is God, and as far as I
can tell, God loves us all, no matter what.

God's plan works 100% of the time.

Living in the moment...
satisfaction guaranteed!

There's never a dull moment when you're in the moment.

The truth about anger is that this is going to hurt me more than it hurts you.

The ego is merely a mirage; it is not real. It just appears to
be real.

History will repeat itself unless we raise our level of consciousness.

Moods can change as quickly as clouds parting in the sky,
but truth is always shining through like the sun.

Truth is like music to the ears, vibrating through the soul.

Truth is not popular because we have to stop blaming the outside for our problems.   Our reality is created from the inside out.

If you don't have anything nice to think about, then don't think at all.

If you listen to your intuition, you'll be in the right position for your dreams to come to fruition.

An emotional wound can never heal if it's constantly reopened by psychologically picking at it.

Time spent in the calmness of your mind is never a waste
of time.   On the contrary, it's the wisest use of time.

We don't need to re-program our minds,
we just need to un-program the false beliefs, and then our
original positive programming can shine through.

No matter what song is playing in your life today, you may as well sing along, because it's just more fun that way.

Judgement is a thief robbing us of our own experience.

If we persecute ourselves for our past "mistakes," we will be useless in the present for ourselves and others.

Like a photograph, we are only seeing an image of life, and we have a software like photoshop that can alter the image...it's called our belief system.

It is preferable to prevent a bad mood than to have to get out of one after the fact. However, one can always change their mood at any time by what thoughts they put their energy into.

The best feelings are the ones we came into this world
with.

Where do problems go when we are not thinking about them, Never-never land?

It doesn't make sense to put conditions on love.   It's either unconditional love, or it's not love.

When we feel grateful, everything looks like a blessing. When we are ungrateful, those same things look like a curse.

The Ego's job is to doubt and argue, amongst other things, because it originates from fear.

You can't paint a picture of a city from the first floor of a skyscraper.

It's easy as an adult to think that we have lost our innocence. Not true, we are innocence.

Most people aren't afraid of dying; they're afraid of living.

We are all searching for Truth, whether we realize it or not. There are many ways to search for Truth but only one place to find it. Truth lies within.

We can start feeling love out of the blue, and it radiates throughout our being.   Then, we might realize how beautiful life really is and how good it feels to just be ourselves.

The Snowball Effect of Insights is when we start getting insights and the momentum keeps carrying forward until you realize you have a big snowball of wisdom.

The mind is like a grocery store with a built-in health food section and an acquired junk food section.
Choose wisely, and we are rewarded with abundance.

Victories towards love and understanding are always a huge blessing for humanity.

Life's challenges are there to showcase the human spirit's ability to triumph.

Thinking too hard stifles the creative process.

If old beliefs that don't serve us anymore hang around too long, they begin to crowd our minds. Take time to clear the way for a new way of thinking.

Just like a superhero needs a suit to deflect bullets, we need to wear our HAPPINESS SUIT to deflect life's problems.

Throw away negative thoughts just like you would rotten eggs, and for the same reason...they stink.

We seek truth, whether we know it or not in various ways. The common denominator is that they are giving you a roadmap to look within. If this happens, then a spiritual awakening occurs, and your level of consciousness rises. This is the only way and the real solution to human suffering. There only appears to be several ways to do this.

When the volume of our internal gibberish gets so loud, we can't hear the gentle inner voice coming from our wisdom.

Once we see what is true, we also see what is false.

You could have everything you want in this world, but without gratitude, you have nothing.

You could have very little materially, but if you have gratitude, you feel like you're rich.

When we are in gratitude, the cup looks half full, and when we are ungrateful, the cup looks half empty. Either way, the same amount of water is in the cup.

Gratitude cleanses the soul.

It's just as easy to find something to be grateful for as it is to find something to complain about.   They both require the same amount of effort.

THINK without thinking.

The human spirit is alive and well.   It can triumph over anything.

Being grateful to life itself is an amazing feeling.

If you swim towards a waterfall, you might fall off.

We are the very essence of pure positivity.

If we want to be happy today, we must make it a priority. We take ownership of our own mood.   We can't blame our past, the future, other people, our circumstances, etc., knowing that truth sets us free!

Love heals all psychological wounds.

Give yourself permission to experience what it is to be worthy of all the greatest gifts life has to offer. We are born worthy of abundance.

You can lead someone to the light, and then it's up to them to witness it by looking within.

If we play with the tough guys on the playground, we might get hurt. Likewise, if we wrestle with our negative thoughts, we might hurt ourselves.

Allow yourself to be touched by the beauty of life.

The state of meditation is more important than the act of meditation.

Marinate yourself in good feelings.

When a bird hatches, it is happy to be free of that confining eggshell. Then it notices that even though the nest is nice and cozy, there is a whole other world out there. Once the bird realizes it has wings and was meant to soar, it takes a risk and flies. The sky's the limit.

Go to the Spirit of the Universe and get your free Spiritual Upgrade.

It's your birthright and available every day of your life! It's highly recommended.

Life is an expression of Divine Love.

Speak from your soul, and the words will flow out of your mouth without thinking about it. Communication becomes effortless.

You don't have to change your job, your house, your car, your spouse, or your friends and family. Just change your ATTITUDE, and all those things will appear to have changed.

Warning - Spiritual ignorance is bad for your health.

Being in Love has to be the best feeling on earth. Love for life, love for your spouse, love for your children, love for family and friends, love for humanity, love for yourself, and of course, love for God.

Every day is sunny with a chance of clouds. The clouds being my old belief system, and the sun being natural innate health.

It's kind of like our employer, The Spirit of the Universe, said: "Why are you using a PC with a DOS operating system, don't you know there is a computer called a MAC that is much more user friendly?"

Using the intellect for matters that require WISDOM is like using a saw to hammer a nail.

Going back into the past to fix the present makes no sense.
If you have ever been truly present, you would notice a
"Presence." This "Presence" is perfection itself and
doesn't need to be fixed.

Don't let your thoughts cloud up your sunshine.

Have you had a "Soul Burst" lately? It is a spontaneous, amazingly beautiful feeling rising from your spirit for no apparent reason.

God's job...run the universe.

Our job...enjoy God's creation.

It's that simple.

Treat negative thoughts the same way you would an undesirable stray cat. Don't feed it, and it won't hang around.

Practice the art of meditation without meditating.

Once we let go of our old beliefs about life and who we are, what we are left with is PURE POTENTIAL. It's an awesome feeling to realize you don't know who you are anymore or what's possible in life. The possibilities become limitless.

Ordinary people can do amazing things when they lose
their fear of success.

The mental forecast calls for happiness with a chance of some bad thoughts.

The state of meditation can be achieved anywhere, whereas the act of meditating can only be done in certain places and certain positions.

Let negative thoughts float by like clouds in the sky.

There is a radical new concept in the mental health field. It's called "YOU ARE NOT BROKEN; YOU DON'T NEED TO BE FIXED." Check it out for yourself; you might find out they are right!

If everyone found inner peace, there would be world peace.

On a spiritual plane, we are all equal. Every person is full of wisdom.

We are our own best teachers.

Once the seed of insight has been planted, spiritual growth is inevitable, and life begins to blossom.

Dear Creator, I am thankful for my life, and I'm in love with the life you have provided me. I accept life exactly the way it is today. My life is not perfect, but life itself is perfection.

There is no better place in the world than being in "the Now." We take it with us wherever we go.

Truth is so profoundly simple it's easy to miss.

We are all sitting on gold mines of pure potential, whether we realize it or not. All of us are deeply rich in terms of beautiful feelings.

If it ain't broke, don't fix it! We are not broken, so there is
nothing to fix!

When God calls you to be part of the team, cast your doubts and fears aside, so you can be of greater service to humanity.

Waking up spiritually is like waking up from a bad dream; you realize it was just a dream, and it wasn't real. It was just our thinking that caused us to believe something was real – it's not truth.

Today is a great day to choose to be happy!

We are all bonded by God's eternal **love**.

As the mind clears, the heart's playground opens its doors.

Here's a great get-rich-quick scheme. Count all your blessings then ask yourself if you feel rich.

Happiness is way too important not to be a top priority.
It's like insulation for life.

Being in the moment is the full meal deal...the whole enchilada. When we are present, we can witness the little gifts in life. We can see the preciousness of life.

Nobody plays the game of life perfectly. We are all innocently doing the best we can. That's all part of this human condition we are in.

Marinate yourself in gratitude, and you'll get a fresh new perspective on life because you've just been tenderized.

If Guilt and his sidekick, Shame, show up at your party, show them to the door immediately. Those two party-poopers can ruin an otherwise beautiful party because those thoughts stink.

People who do great things do so because they simply know they are worthy of greatness.

Heaven is that amazing beautiful feeling that lies within all of us.

If you love life, it will love you back.

Practice being while doing.

Inside everyone is a very special toolbox. Only we have the key to it. If you open it up, you will find everything you need: love, abundance, joy, resiliency, gratitude, and forgiveness, to name a few.

Life is too precious to waste time on fruitless activities.
Our wisdom guides us towards that which produces fruit.

If you pick a scab, you'll be right back where you started.

We don't have to believe a thought is true just because it pops into our minds.

Crazy ideas are harmless if we don't act on them.

There is no thought in our head more important than the Truth in our soul.

Swimming upstream against the current takes a lot of effort, and you end up going nowhere. May as well just turn around and see where the current takes you.

We don't have to choose just one day of the week to be happy. We can choose happiness all seven days of the week!

The miracle is in seeing the miracle.

Human beings get out of tune, just like musical instruments. When this happens, we need to get back in tune with the frequency of love.

What's inside? It's beautiful, it's always available, it can't be broken, it can't be touched...it can only be experienced.

No metaphor or analogy is perfect. There is no perfect metaphor or analogy to explain Truth. There will always be an argument or loophole seen by the intellect. Only the soul can see beyond the metaphor or analogy to see Truth.

It doesn't take years to find Truth. It takes a split second.
That still moment in-between thoughts is all it takes.

Make regular dates with God; you will never be stood up. Whenever we truly seek God, we are always met with Love.

Boredom: "Same crap, different day," or is it really "Same thoughts, different day?"

It's not your fault, nor anyone else's. You are not to blame, nor is anyone else. We are all innocent when it comes to our behaviors, habits, problems, etc.

We are all on the same team; we just wear different uniforms.

The story of our life was already written in our soul. All we must do is open it up to the current page.

Hit the REFRESH button; it is there. Sometimes we forget
we have one and where to find it.

The path has already been paved. Try walking on it; there
will be less resistance.

It is pretty reassuring to realize there is an ever-present beautiful feeling within all of us that cannot be damaged.

If worrying were your weatherman, he would say there's a chance of a tornado or maybe a hailstorm or possibly even torrential rains. In any case, terrible weather is imminent. When that guy comes on, change the channel. He's not a very good weatherman.

A man was granted one wish from a genie in a bottle. The man asked for a conversation with God. The genie granted the wish. The man asked God why he was never shown a sign when he had prayed for it every day. God replied, "My dear child, I gave you a sign; it is you, so hold your sign up high, be proud of it, and show it to the rest of the world."

If you get out of your head, you'll know what's to be said.

Feeling carefree doesn't mean you don't care.

You are more than a star in the universe; you are the universe.

Everything comes from a land that has no form.

The good news...life is what you make of it! The bad
news...life is what you make of it.

Beautiful and fulfilling destinies are for everyone, not just a select few.

The answer is so close. Just remove whatever thought is bothering you, and what pops up in its place without effort that feels good is what you're looking for.

God has already moved on. Have you?

It doesn't matter what the problem is, the answer is always the same.

Most things in life are *matters of the soul*, **not** matters of the intellect.

About the Author

Bryan D. Johnson is an author who lives in Denver, Colorado. He has worked in both business and education.

Over the past five years, since having a transformational experience while at Gulf Breeze Recovery, he has helped others by sharing his story and writing quotes online.

Visit Bryan at BryanDJohnson.com for contact information, services, and upcoming events.

CPSIA information can be obtained
at www.ICGtesting.com
Printed in the USA
LVHW081338180921
698140LV00027B/1101